LOST LINES OF WALES
BANGOR TO AFON WEN

PAUL LAWTON
DAVID SOUTHERN

GRAFFEG

CONTENTS

FOREWORD

The line from Bangor to Afon Wen is one of the most interesting of the lost lines of Wales. It is still remembered with great affection by many local residents and railway enthusiasts. It was one that both authors were acquainted with – one travelled on it as a child in the line's heyday; the other travelled on the last train on the truncated section from Bangor to Caernarvon (as the name was then spelt by British Railways), a rather more poignant occasion.

The journey started from Bangor and then continued along the strategically important north Wales coastal line to Menai Bridge. It parted company with the main line before the Britannia Bridge, departing in a southwesterly direction alongside the Menai Strait heading for Caernarfon. Thereafter there were no towns to generate much in the way of passenger traffic as the line meandered its way through the delightful Llŷn peninsula till it reached the sea at Afon Wen. It was a pleasant journey and also of great interest because of its history.

It was not strictly speaking a branch line, but like many similar routes in Wales it gave all the impression of being one. It was a typical Welsh rural railway with much of its business conducted in the Welsh language, a fact that caused some controversy in the past. The issue arose in 1895 because of a circular issued by W. Dawson of the Permanent Way Department at Bangor to his inspectors, which read:

'Notwithstanding my instructions on this subject, I find that a number of men have been taken on who cannot speak English, or who can only speak English a little. The services of such men unable to speak English are to be dispensed with.'

This effectively excluded a large number of the local population from employment on the railway. The controversy that ensued and which reflects very badly on the London & North Western Railway rumbled on for a number of years and was actually raised in Parliament. Lloyd George promised to sort it out if he was elected to Parliament but never did so.

This brings the authors to the issue of how the railway companies of the past tended to anglicise the Welsh names of the places they served. Their solution has been to use the proper Welsh name when referring to a place and to use the contemporary railway spellings in company and station titles. Even then, these were not consistent and changed with the passing of the years.

BRITISH RAILWAYS

RUN-ABOUT TICKETS
(Go-As-You-Please)

IN

NORTH WALES

ISSUED UNTIL OCTOBER 28th, 1949

Available for Five Days
Monday to Friday inclusive

UNRESTRICTED TRAVEL WITHIN THE AREA
BY ANY TRAIN

AREA No. 1 covers :—
Prestatyn, Rhyl, Denbigh, Ruthin, Abergele, Colwyn Bay, Llandudno, Llanrwst, Bettws-y-Coed, Blaenau Festiniog, Bangor, Bethesda, Caernarvon, Afonwen, Amlwch, Holyhead and all intermediate Stations Also Llanberis during the Season

15/-

THIRD CLASS

CHILDREN UNDER 14 HALF-FARE

AREA No. 7 covers :—
Chester, Holywell Town, Rhyl, Abergele, Denbigh, Mold, Ffrith, Corwen, Colwyn Bay, Llandudno, Conway, Penmaenmawr, Llanfairfechan, and all intermediate Stations

BICYCLE TICKETS - 8·2   DOG TICKETS - 4·2
issued in conjunction with the above for five days.

PANORAMA MAP OF NORTH WALES — SEE INSIDE

TICKETS OBTAINABLE AT ANY STATION WITHIN THE AREA

The Bangor to Afon Wen line was very much a railway of two halves, important towns in the first part, sleepy countryside in the second. It was also a railway composed of many pieces, different parts constructed at different times by different undertakings. The railway arrived in Bangor on 1st May 1848, when the town became the first western terminus of the Chester & Holyhead Railway. It was to remain the terminus for two years pending the completion of the Britannia Tubular Bridge across the Menai Straits. At first there were just four trains running each way daily, though the route when completed was to be of great importance, sufficiently so to attract government money. It received a subsidy of £30,000 a year for the carriage of mails. This was an unusual occurrence at the time since governments of the period were particularly reluctant to spend money in any way. They were, however, keen to solve a strategic problem, that of the link with Ireland. Following the Act of Union with Ireland in 1800, communication between London and Dublin became of prime importance. The British government first solved the problem by commissioning Thomas Telford to engineer the great 'Holyhead Road' that today we know as the A5, a solution that lasted only as long as the dawning of the railway age. It was a sadly short-lived triumph for Telford, the 'colossus of roads' as the poet Southey nicknamed him. The road was not fully complete until 1826, just four years before the Liverpool to Manchester Railway opened. Within less than a decade plans were being laid for a railway that would supersede the road and render the horse-drawn mail coach obsolete. It was to be almost a century before motor transport came to challenge the supremacy of the railways and Telford's masterpiece came into its own.

The first railway to arrive in Caernarfon existed some years before a line reached Bangor when an Act of Parliament incorporated the Nantlle Railway in May 1825. This was engineered to deliver copper and slates from the Nantlle Valley down a 9-mile tramway to Caernarfon quayside via Penygroes. Although not especially early for this type of horse-drawn tramway to be constructed since their history went back centuries, it was a notable line for several reasons. Firstly, George and Robert Stephenson, those great father-and-son luminaries of railway development, were involved. They were engaged to lay the rails though not to engineer the line and felt that the gauge should have been wider, committed as they were to their choice of 4ft 8½in that was destined to become our standard gauge. Secondly, the Nantlle branch survived into the era of British Railways, at which time it became the object of much interest and affection amongst railway enthusiasts. By then it was the only 3ft 6in-gauge track in their ownership and was destined to be the last of the very few horse-drawn lines that they inherited on the nationalisation of the railways in 1948. It survived on into the 1960s, by which time the long-suffering horses were the subject of countless feet of cine film and endless photographs taken by railway enthusiasts. The section that remained at that point was just the length nearest the quarries. The Nantlle's route to the coast was a good one and it attracted the attention of the promoters of the Carnarvonshire Railway, which

had been authorised to construct a railway from Caernarfon to Porthmadog. Hence the first 6 miles or so of the Nantlle were rebuilt as a single-track line between Caernarfon and Penygroes in 1866, and the extension southwards to join the Cambrian Railways at Afon Wen opened the following year. The northern section connecting Caernarfon with Bangor required two further pieces of the jigsaw to become complete.

The first standard gauge line to reach Caernarfon was opened for passenger traffic from Menai Bridge station by the Bangor & Carnarvon Railway on 1st July 1852. It had opened for the all-important mineral traffic between Menai Bridge and Port Dinorwic in the previous March. Despite the completion of the line south to Afon Wen in 1867, there was still no possibility of a through service to Bangor until 5th July 1870 when the Caernarvon town line was brought into use. This line also provided a connection to the Carnarvon & Llanberis Railway, which had opened on 1st July 1869. Thus was completed the line that is the subject of this book, a somewhat complicated slice of railway history that had led to Caernarfon having three separate railway stations. Though valiant examples of Victorian enterprise, this plethora of small companies was almost an irrelevance from the start, given their susceptibility to takeover and the rapacious appetite of the larger concerns, in particular the London & North Western Railway. The latter worked the C&HR from the start and took it over completely in 1859. In the end the LNWR absorbed all the small concerns that had been responsible for building the railway from Bangor to Afon Wen. In its turn the LNWR was superseded by the London, Midland & Scottish Railway at the Grouping in 1923, which became part of the London Midland Region of British Railways at the time of nationalisation in 1948.

Construction of the line from Caernarfon to Afon Wen was overseen by Thomas Savin, a well-known figure in the development of Welsh railways and a gentleman whose name is commemorated in the name of a road in Oswestry. He often took a gamble when it came to railway affairs and sometimes he took a step too far. On 6th September 1866, by which time Savin was

actually bankrupt, the railway ran an excursion from Porthmadog to Caernarvon stations even though the line still lacked Board of Trade approval. It is unclear whether Savin promoted this jaunt or disapproved of it, but the result was an accident. This was one of a number of excursions the railway had decided to run in the interval between completion of the works and full approval of them. The Carnarvonshire Volunteers had thus been catered for, as had a church group going on an outing. So when the citizens of Pwllheli and Porthmadog requested a train be run so that they could attend a Calvinist meeting in Caernarfon, the railway was keen to oblige. A trip was organised even though no suitable stock was available. A train was put together that consisted of a locomotive and twenty ballast wagons fitted out with benches, a provision that gave scant protection to passengers in a derailment. The train left Porthmadog at six in the morning and ran up the line without incident, though it became clear that not everyone was fully aware of the arrangement, there having been some breakdown in communication. The return working departed from Carnarvon Pant station (one of the town's three) at 7.00pm. As was often the case in these things, it was a dark and stormy night, and the train stopped short of Brynkir station to take on water. After it did so, it set off again. The points had been set so that the train would take the west line of the loop past the station as there was a wagon standing on the east line. As it crossed over the points that formed the north end of the passing loop the engine went one way and the tender and wagons went another. The result was that the engine came off the rails on one line and four trucks were derailed on the other. Three of them turned over, killing five people and mortally wounding a sixth. The cause of the accident was given as a stone lodged in the points. The accident could have been prevented if the point lever had been held in position by a pointsman, but no instruction to do so had been given. At the coroner's inquest the presence of the stone was blamed on a malicious act, and a reward was offered for the apprehension of an offender. The Board of Trade inspector, however, did not agree that it was a malicious act, being of the opinion that the stone had fallen into the points during works to the line. In any event, the Company was not held to be responsible.

One of the great delights of the Bangor-Afon Wen line was the variety of motive power that was employed on it. If we go back to LNWR days, in addition to the usual 2-4-2 and 0-6-2 tanks and 0-6-0s, medium and large tender engines were often used on the line. Sometimes there was a real rarity. On 13th July 1911, on the occasion of the Investiture of the Prince of Wales at Caernarfon Castle, the LNWR Royal Train was hauled to a temporary station at Griffiths Crossing, near Caernarfon, by two of the then-new superheated 4-6-2 tank engines. The 1923 Grouping produced few changes and the LNWR stock continued in use as before, with Prince of Wales class 4-6-0 locomotives hauling many of the Bangor-Afon Wen services. The so-called Coal Tank 0-6-2 tank class designed by F. W. Webb together with other LNWR locomotives survived into the BR era. One notable survivor was Coal Tank No 58903 that was still working out of Bangor shed in the early 1950s. These were gradually replaced by more modern designs such as the class 2 mixed traffic 2-6-2 tanks designed by H. G. Ivatt. One of these, No 41200, became a favourite at Bangor shed, though judging by contemporary photographs its status did not mean it was kept in any cleaner condition than its stable mates. It may or may not be true that the shed master, Mr Dunn, would tip his hat to the locomotive each morning as he passed the time of day with it; what is more sure is that he always chose to have it in the background when he was photographed. It may have been a question of familiarity. The engine was at Bangor for nearly all its working life.

The line was injected with new life when Butlins opened a holiday camp at Penychain, near Pwllheli, in 1947. During the summer season through trains travelled along the north Wales coastal line to Bangor and then along the route to Afon Wen via Caernarfon. Some came from as far as Euston, including the named train *The Welshman*, which ran from London to Llandudno and Portmadoc, or Pwllheli. This service was originally introduced by the London Midland & Scottish Railway in 1927 as a summer-only restaurant car express to link the capital with the popular north Wales seaside resorts. The service was suspended during the Second World War but reappeared in 1950. According to the 1962 timetable the Monday to Friday Down service left Euston at 11.20am and, after calling at Rugby and Crewe, arrived in Chester at 3.26pm, where the train was divided. The Llandudno portion called at resorts along the north Wales coast before arriving at its destination at 5.03pm. The second portion travelled non-stop to Penmaenmawr, calling at Llanfairfechan and then Bangor for a change of engine. It was usually a Fairburn 2-6-4 tank from Bangor shed that took over the rest of the journey. At Afon Wen the train was split again into coaches for Portmadoc and coaches for Pwllheli. The Up service back to London left Pwllheli at 10.00am on weekdays, reaching London at 6.35pm. One can only hope that the holiday was enjoyable enough to justify the endurance required for the journey.

The late 1950s and the 1960s were years of decline for the Bangor-Afon Wen route, just as they were for many parts of the railway network. The election of a Conservative government in 1951 meant there was a reversal of the previously pro-railway policies. The end of petrol rationing and increased prosperity brought an increase in both private and commercial motor transport. As car ownership increased in the 1950s, traffic levels declined on the Afon Wen route as it did on many rural lines throughout the country. Costs, especially wage costs, were outstripping revenue and neither the government nor the electorate were prepared to take a long-term view of the value of the railway network and subsidise it further. The 1963 publication of the disingenuously titled report *The Reshaping of British Railways* sounded the death knell for much of the rural railway network, including the Bangor-Afon Wen line. The section from Caernarfon to Afon Wen was consigned to the dustbin of history from Monday, 7th December 1964. The section between Menai Bridge and Caernarfon remained in operation with a diesel multiple unit operated service of nine trains each way to and from Bangor. The section proved of use during the Investiture of the Prince of Wales in July 1969, but such a truncated spur was unlikely to survive for long. This section of the line was closed with effect from Monday, 5th January 1970, with the last trains being run on the proceeding Saturday. It was on the very last train that one of the authors was privileged to travel.

In some respects the Afon Wen route has survived remarkably well, given that many rural railways disappear back into the landscape with scarcely a trace after closure. Some 12 miles of the trackbed between Caernarfon and Bryncir have been reopened as a footpath and cycleway known as Lôn Eifion. Since 2000 the section north of Dinas has been joined by the revitalised Welsh Highland Railway, which from 2011 has operated narrow-gauge trains between Caernarfon and Porthmadog. A fence separates trains from the pedestrians and walkers who are served by a halt at Bontnewydd.

Like many rural lines, the Afon Wen route was the butt of some humour. One of the best-wrought pieces appeared in the *Caernarvon and Denbigh Herald* in January 1957, sent in by an unknown author following the closure of Pant Glâs station:

If you've travelled down from Bangor,
More in sorrow than in anger,
To Pwllheli in a British Railways train,
Or to Bangor from the latter,
For direction does not matter,
And are doomed to do the journey yet again,
If you've tarried at Caernarvon
In a train you've slowly starved on,
If you've sat while boys beside you grew to men,
And before you reach Llanwnda,
Have indeed began to wonder
If you'd live to see the lights of Afon Wen,
If you've started to rejoice
At the sight of Penygroes,
Then remembered all the stations yet ahead,
If you've thought, when tired of staring,
At the wristwatch you are wearing,
That you should have brought a calendar instead,

And it seemed that Brynkir halt you'd never pass
Here's a spot of news to brace you
For the journey still to face you,
Henceforth you won't be stopping at Pant Glâs.

On that light-hearted note, it is time to begin our journey, in photographs at least, down the line from Bangor to Afon Wen. We are privileged to see some of the journey from the footplate of different steam locomotives thanks to the excellent photographs taken at the time by Norman Kneale.

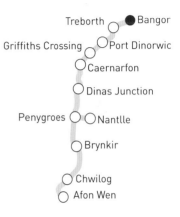

Treborth ○ ●Bangor

Griffiths Crossing ○ ○ Port Dinorwic

○ Caernarfon

○ Dinas Junction

Penygroes ○ ○ Nantlle

○ Brynkir

○ Chwilog

○ Afon Wen

We begin our journey at a station that is very far from being lost or forgotten. Bangor was, and still is, the principal station between Llandudno Junction and Holyhead on the important north Wales coastal line. Many of the Holyhead and London trains stop here just as they did when there were still trains departing for Afon Wen. Francis Thompson designed the original station and the contractor was a Mr Morris of Birkenhead. It was planned so that fast through trains could overtake stopping trains standing at the platforms, but as traffic developed it became obvious that improvements would have to be made. After the railways were grouped into four main concerns in 1923 and the London, Midland & Scottish Railway took control, a plan was quickly put into effect to provide an additional through platform, a new overbridge and generally improved facilities. By 1952 the station was dealing with over

81,000 tons of freight, including 21,000 tons of outgoing mineral traffic, as well as issuing over 80,000 passenger tickets; as such it was a vital railhead for a large rural hinterland.

Our first image shows the main entrance to Bangor station. On the left is the booking hall and to the right are the parcels office and cloakrooms. Old and new transport is visible in the distance in the form of a vintage motor vehicle and a horse drawn carriage, illustrating the dramatic transition that occurred in the early years of the 20th century.

BANGOR, CAERNARVON, LLANBERIS, NANTLLE AND AFONWEN.

WEEKDAYS.

	Miles		1 PARCELS 1.30 a.m. from Chester. (T.P. & SO)	2 PASSENGER	3 MOTOR TRAIN	5 PASSENGER	6 MOTOR TRAIN	7 MOTOR TRAIN	8 PASSENGER	10 MOTOR TRAIN	11 PASSENGER	12 PASSENGER 6.9 a.m. from Prestatyn	13 PASSENGER 9.0 a.m. from Chester	14 PASSENGER 10.0 a.m. from Llandudno	15 PASSENGER	16 PASSENGER 7.20 a.m. from Manchester	17 MOTOR TRAIN	19 PASSENGER 7.38 a.m. from Manchester (Ex. 9.3 a.m. from Chester (SO))	20 MOTOR TRAIN	21 PASSENGER	23 MOTOR TRAIN	24 PASSENGER	25 MOTOR TRAIN	26 PASSENGER 12.33 a.m. from Llandudno Jn.	27 PASSENGER	29 MOTOR TRAIN	30 PASSENGER	22 EXPRESS 11.18 a.m. from Manchester	34	35 PASSENGER	36 MOTOR TRAIN	38 MOTOR TRAIN	40 PASSENGER 11.18 a.m. from Manchester	41 MOTOR TRAIN
			a.m.	a.m.	a.m.	a.m.			a.m.		S a.m.	S a.m.	S a.m.	S a.m.	a.m.	a.m.	a.m.		p.m.	p.m.		S p.m.	p.m.	SO p.m.	S p.m.	SO p.m.	S p.m.	S		p.m.	p.m.	p.m.	S p.m.	SO p.m.
		BANGOR ....dep.	4 15	4 46	...	6 45	...	...	8 55	...	10 26	10 36	10 41	...	11 13	...	11 24	12 2	12 5	...	12 15	...	1 13	1 14	1 23	...	1 30	...	...	2 2	2 13	2 20
1½		Menai Bridge.... .. arr.	4 18	4 49	...	6 48	...	...	8 58	...	10 29	10 39	10 44	...	11 16	...	11 27	12 5	12 6	...	12 18	...	1 16	1 17	1 26	...	...	...	...	2 5	2 16	2 23
2½		Treborth .. .. dep.	...	K	...	6 49	...	...	9 1	...	10 30	10 40	10 45	...	11 17	...	11 28	12 6	12 6	...	12 19	...	1 17	1 19	1 27	...	33	...	...	2 6	3 13	2 24
4½		Port Dinorwic	...	4 55	...	K	...	...	9 4	...	10 43	...	...	...	11 20	...	11 31	...	K	...	K	...	1 20	1 22	1 30	...	...	...	...	2 9	...	K
6½		Griffith's Crossing	...	...	...	6 57	...	...	9 9	...	10 48	...	...	...	11 25	...	11 36	12 14	...	...	12 27	...	1 25	1 27	1 35	...	...	...	...	2 14	...	2 32
8½	0	CAERNARVON ⊕ ⊕ arr.	4 30	5 4	...	7 7	...	...	9 14	...	10 53	...	...	...	11 30	...	K	...	...	...	1 30	...	1 30	1 38	1 40	...	...	...	...	2 19	...	K
		CAERNARVON ⊕ ⊕ dep.	4 35	5 14	...	7 10	6 49	7 50	9 24	...	10 43	10 58	10 56	...	11 35	...	11 45	11 51	...	12 29	12 40	...	12 41	4	...	...	1 38	1 51	2 5	...	...	2 24	2 26	2 44
3½		Pont Rug ....dep.					7 0		9 45																1 0								
5½		Pontrhythallt .⊕. dep.					7 5		9 50														1 5		1 5	1 20						2*16	
6½		Cwm-y-Glo .⊕. dep.	See note			7 6	8 4		9 51	10 58	11 20	11 13					11 57		See note	1 10				1 10	1 25								
9		LLANBERIS .⊕. arr.			7 10	8 8		9 55											See note	1 14				1 14	1 29						2*24		See note
							7 14	8 12	9 59	11 5	11 27	11 20					12 4																	
11½		Dinas Junction ⊕ ⊕ arr.	4*56	5*25	...	7 20	...	...	9 34	...	...	...	...	11 14	...	...	12 1	...	...	12 39	...	12 51	...	...	1 48	2 1	...	...	...	2 36	2 53	2 54
12½		Llanwnda .. .. dep.		5*28	...	7 23	...	...	9 35	...	...	...	...	...	...	...	12 2	...	...	12 52	...	12 52	...	...	1 49	2 2	...	...	...	...	2A30	2 58
13		Groeslon ⊕ ⊕ arr.	5 1	...	...	7 26	...	...	9 38	...	...	...	...	...	...	...	12 2	...	...	12 43	...	12 55	...	...	2 0	2 9	...	...	...	...	...	3 0
		Groeslon ⊕ ⊕ dep.	5 2	5 32	...	7 27	...	...	9 42	...	...	...	...	...	...	...	12 0	...	...	12 59	...	...	...	...	...	...	...	...	...	2*43	3 3	3
15½	0	PENYGROES ⊕ ⊕ arr.	5 6	5 37	...	7 32	8 24	...	9 47	10 0	...	...	...	...	...	...	12 52	...	...	12 52	...	1 0	...	...	1 55	2 11	...	...	...	2 48	3 8
		PENYGROES ⊕ ⊕ dep.	5 10	5 40	7 40	7 34	8 25	...	9 48	10 0	...	...	...	10 35	...	...	12 15	12 57	12 54	12 15	1 20	1 8	...	...	2 0	2 16	...	...	...	2 51	3 11
19½	1½	NANTLLE ⊕ ⊕ arr.	...	...	7 45	...	8 30	...	...	10 5	...	...	...	10 40	...	11 50	...	1 2	...	12 20	1 25	...	...	2 0	...	2 6	...	...	3 0	3 16
21		Pant Glas .. .. dep.	...	...	...	7 44	...	...	9 58	...	...	...	...	...	12 25	...	1 4	...	...	...	...	...	...	...	...	2 38	...	...	...
23		Brynkir .. .. ⊕ arr.	5 24	5 54	...	7 47	...	...	10 1	...	...	...	...	...	12 28	...	1 7	...	...	1 18	...	...	...	...	...	2 39	...	3 3	...
		Ynys .. .. ⊕ dep.	5 25	5 55	...	7 48	...	...	10 6	...	...	...	...	...	12 29	...	1 10	...	...	1 20	...	...	...	...	...	...	...	...	...
24½		Llangybi .. .. ⊕ dep.	5*32	...	...	7 54	...	...	10 10	...	...	...	...	...	12 33	...	1 14	...	...	...	...	...	...	...	...	...	...	...	...
		Chwilog .. .. ⊕ dep.	5 36	6 2	...	7 56	...	...	10 13	...	...	...	...	...	12 41	...	1 23	...	...	1 26	...	...	...	...	...	2*45	...	3*0	...
26		Chwilog .. .. ⊕ dep.		6 4	...	7 59	...	...	10 16	...	...	...	...	...	12 43	...	1 25	...	...	1 28	...	...	...	...	...	2 47	...	3 11	...
27½		AFONWEN .. .. arr.	5 37	6 8	...	8 1	...	...	10 17	...	...	...	...	...	12 45	...	1 28	...	...	1 32	...	...	...	...	...	2 48	...	3 12	...
		AFONWEN .. .. arr.	5 40	6 8	...	8 4	...	...	10 20	...	...	...	...	...	12 48	...	1 31	...	...	...	...	...	...	...	...	2 51	...	3 15	...

Passenger Trains cannot cross at Pontrhythallt and Chwilog

No. 1—Runs daily empty stock, between Caernarvon and Afonwen.

Nos. 32 and 40—A—Calls at Llanwnda if required to set down passengers from Manchester.

Nos. 5, 17, 20, 24, 41—K—Calls at Treborth and Griffith's Crossing to set down passengers on notice to guard at preceding stopping station, and to pick up passengers on notice at the Station.

Bangor station itself, like many others in Wales, was constricted by the confines of the site upon which it was constructed being hemmed in by two hills. There are thus two tunnels, one on either side of the station, with Bangor tunnel to the east and Belmont tunnel to the west. Into the restricted area were crammed the passenger station, a goods depot, an engine shed and the civil engineer's department. Here we see ex-LMS Black 5 4-6-0 No 44917 alongside the island platform at Bangor while a class 101 DMU sits on the other side ready for a local service to Holyhead.

The north Wales main line engine sheds were busy places. In the 1950s the number of locomotives allocated to Bangor was always well over 20 and all required maintenance and preparation. The number of people employed at Bangor in the past was large. In 1953 211 worked for the Motive Power Department alone and that figure excluded office staff. Of that number 40 were named Williams and 31 were Jones. In addition there were around 260 engineering staff employed at the Bangor based District Civil Engineer's headquarters. The railway was therefore a major employer, generating at the height of the steam era some 560 jobs including the station staff. Over the years the shed code for Bangor changed. Having started life in London & North Western days as number 21, it became number 7B under the LMS in 1935. British Railways reclassified it as 6H in 1952

and it was that number that it retained until closure on 12th June 1965, when just 15 locomotives remained.

In this image we see ex-LMS Black 5 4-6-0 No 44917 backing into the shed. In the background the water tower stands over a siding while on the right are carriage sidings and the goods shed with a class 40 and an early diesel shunter. On the left a parcel train stands by the island platform and a ballast train is in the shed yard.

Ex-LMS 2-6-4 tank engine No 42157 speeds along the main line with a vintage rake of coaches for Afon Wen in 1956. The locomotive has a 6H shed plate on the smokebox door, denoting that the engine was allocated to Bangor Motive Power Depot. The train's next stop would have been Menai Bridge, the first station encountered on the route down to Afon Wen. The station at Menai Bridge is now closed, though the section of line from Bangor that once served it is still open, forming part of the important route to Holyhead. The junction from here leading south to Port Dinorwic was opened on 10th March 1852 by the Bangor & Carnarvon Railway and from 1st July 1852 it opened through to Caernarfon. In the early years the junction saw some interesting train movements since all the branch trains had to reverse on and off the main line before proceeding to Caernarfon,

an arrangement that lasted up until 1865 when an accident encouraged a reassessment. Menai Bridge station was located half-a-mile west of Telford's Suspension Bridge and opened on 1st October 1858. As at Bangor the site was restricted by topography and to fit the station into the location the booking office was on the ground floor. Steps led up to the first floor that was adjacent to the Up (Chester-bound) platform. The building itself was quite grand and rather Tudoresque in design and was once again the work of the architect Francis Thompson. It was something of a loss when it was demolished on closure.

Jubilee 4-6-0 No 45663 *Jervis*, carrying the reporting number 1C90, leaves the Afon Wen line by Menai Bridge Station signal box with a train from the Butlin's holiday camp at Penychain, near Pwllheli, on the Cambrian Coast line. The station's island platform is visible in the centre of the picture, as is the loading gauge for traffic from the goods yard. Since there was no space for substantial buildings the island platform was provided with a simple shelter that is just visible in the distance behind the wagons.

Once the link through Caernarfon was completed in 1871 and passenger trains ran through to Afon Wen, Menai Bridge became a much busier place since it was an ideal interchange point for passengers wanting to travel between Anglesey and stations along the Afon Wen line. As a result the line between Menai Bridge and Caernarfon was doubled to serve this traffic the

following year. In July 1922 there were 23 Up and 19 Down trains on Mondays to Saturdays, but only one in each direction on Sundays.

After it was closed to passengers on 14th February 1966 and lost its goods services on 4th March 1968, Menai Bridge station enjoyed a brief moment of glory on 1st July 1969 when the Royal Train, carrying Prince Charles to his Investiture as Prince of Wales at Caernarfon, pulled into the station sidings at 3.10am. It remained at the station until just after midday when it set off to complete its journey. After the closure of the Caernarfon line the platforms at Menai Bridge were removed, but the building remained in situ until the 1980s when it was demolished. A children's nursery was later built on the site together with a small industrial estate on the station approach.

TREBORTH

When HM The Queen visited north Wales in August 1963 she used the Royal Train, which was hauled by class 40 diesel No D308 as far as Caernarfon. The train is seen here climbing Treborth bank after leaving Menai Bridge station. On the extreme left is the Bangor-Holyhead main line, while in the centre is the marshalling yard that served the goods trains to Afon Wen.

Treborth station had an interesting history. It was located just 1 mile south of the Menai Bridge junction and 2¼ miles from Bangor in a sparsely populated area. It consisted of one platform with a single-storey building adjacent to the stationmaster's house and owed its existence to a clause inserted into the original land sale agreement with the Bangor & Carnarvon Railway. The vendor, Mary Matilda Crawley, insisted a station must be located at Treborth and

trains must call there in perpetuity. When the LNWR decided to close the station and withdraw services in 1858, they were reminded of the existence of this clause and the service was rapidly reintroduced. By August 1862 there were seven weekday passenger trains running in each direction between Bangor and Caernarfon with three trains on Sundays. Following nationalisation the summer timetable for 1948 showed just two services to Afon Wen, one to Caernarfon and two to Bangor on weekdays. A camping coach was located there for a while in the 1950s but it was never well patronised and was removed after a couple of seasons. The station closed to all traffic on 2nd March 1959; presumably the requirement to provide the station 'in perpetuity' had been cancelled. Treborth station building survives as a private dwelling.

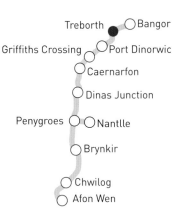

PORT DINORWIC

The story of Port Dinorwic, next stop on the line, is a tale of two stations. The first station in the village of Port Dinorwic (Y Felinheli) was a small station for goods that was opened in 1824 on the Dinorwic Railway, which was later replaced in 1842 by the Padarn Railway. These were built to take slate from the Dinorwic Quarry to the village on narrow gauge lines. The first standard gauge station on the site was that of the Bangor & Carnarvon Railway. A single-track railway opened to Port Dinorwic for goods on 1st March 1852 and for passengers on 10th March 1852. In 1874 the first station at Port Dinorwic closed and was replaced with a new one 200 yards to the south. The new facility was better located, being closer to the centre of the village and the first station was demolished. In its heyday the weekday service consisted of eight northbound and seven southbound departures.

Though Port Dinorwic was quite a large community and the station was conveniently placed to serve it, the main A487 road ran through the village parallel to the railway and there was soon fierce competition from bus services. BR closed the station on 12th September 1960. The goods yard closed in May 1964, with the signalbox closing the following month. Then the unforeseen happened when a fire on the Britannia Bridge in May 1970 isolated Holyhead from the rest of the railway network. Caernarfon was then pressed into service as a freightliner depot, receiving its first trains on 15th June 1970. From that date until 5th February 1972, freightliner services passed through Port Dinorwic. When this ceased the line was closed completely and lifted soon afterwards.

The second station building, a substantial and impressive-looking structure, is pictured here with BR

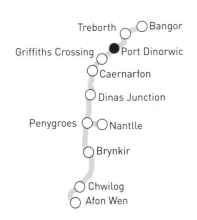

Standard class 4 2-6-4 tank No 80094 running in to the Down platform with a train for Afon Wen sometime in 1957. Fortunately the station survived closure of the line and is now Grade II listed. For some years it was used by Penningtons, a local packaging company, but is now in residential use.

North Wales is renowned for slate production, an industry that was greatly helped by the development of railways. The Bangor-Afon Wen line played an important part in the trade. The slate was found inland and the challenge was to get it to a port for transhipment. At its height the scale of the industry was enormous, as is well illustrated by the vintage photograph of Port Dinorwic harbour reproduced here showing steamers being loaded from stack yards stretching off into the distance and a narrow-gauge locomotive working in the foreground. At one time each quarry owned its own ships as well as narrow-gauge engines and rolling stock, the early tramways down to the quays being the earliest 'railways' in the area.

Port Dinorwic harbour was served by a short branch off the Bangor-Afon Wen line known as Port Siding, just over a mile in length. It left the main line at Port Siding signal box, a little to the north of Port Dinorwic station. The box was of an interesting and impressive appearance, being brick built to a prodigious height to give the signalman a clear view over a nearby road bridge. The last working down to the quay took place on 30th October 1961 and the track was lifted soon afterwards.

Griffiths Crossing, some 6½ miles from Bangor, was another relatively insignificant station in the middle of nowhere, yet it had its moment of glory when it became a station fit for a king. It first appeared in the timetable in June 1854 and took its name from the fact that there was a nearby crossroads. In the years before the Great War Griffiths Crossing was popular with excursions and Sunday school outings and with the Territorial Army, units of which travelled to the station to carry out exercises nearby. The station came into its own at the time of an Investiture at Caernarfon Castle. When the future King Edward VIII was invested as Prince of Wales in 1911, part of the event was a procession into the town led by King George V and Queen Mary and Griffiths Crossing was chosen as the location at which the royal party would alight. They wished to complete their journey by road so that they might be more visible to the crowds. The station facilities were considered inadequate for the royal party, so temporary timber structures were erected which included an extension to the down platform and a canopy. After the event the station reverted to its basic form and a quiet life. The proximity of the main road meant Griffiths Crossing proved vulnerable to road competition and the station lost its passenger services as early as 1937.

On 1st July 1969, Prince Charles was invested as Prince of Wales at Caernarfon Castle. Again, part of the event involved a procession into Caernarfon. As the royal party were to travel to Caernarfon by train, a stopping place was required outside the town. For the 1911 investiture, the Royal Party had stopped at Griffiths Crossing station, which was 2 miles from Caernarfon. Unfortunately the station had closed and the platforms had been demolished and the line from Menai Bridge to Caernarfon was a shadow of its former self. By then the through route to Afon Wen had gone, leaving just the branch to Caernarfon. The solution was to build a temporary platform, at a point slightly closer to Caernarfon than the original Griffiths Crossing station, adjacent to the Ferodo factory. At that point, a bridge crossed the line to the factory, allowing easy main road access. The BR 'Notice of Royal Trains' number 222W referred to the temporary facility as the Ferodo Platform. The platform was a simple construction of about one coach length and a set of steps connected it to the Ferodo factory car park. Once the event was over and the royal party had returned to London, all became quiet once more and the platform was dismantled shortly afterwards.

In our photograph we see the two locomotives (double-heading was de rigueur for royal trains) D233 *Empress of England* and D216 *Campania* stationary at the temporary platform. Nothing was left to chance. Notice the bowler-hatted inspector aboard the leading locomotive, the heavy police presence because of the recent bomb scares and the white post indicating to the driver exactly where to stop. The BBC was also much in evidence. Outside broadcast vehicles are parked to the left of the leading locomotive and a cameraman is ready for a bird's eye view of the proceedings on a crane opposite the platform.

The line's twilight years are captured in this evocative photograph of class 24 diesel D5146 paused at Waterloo Port crossing a short distance from Caernarfon. When the line became freight only and was reduced to just a single track, all the signalling was taken out, so in this view the guard can be seen alighting to open the gates manually. The train consisted of just a brake van. The old gatekeeper's cottage can be seen next to the locomotive.

The main running in board at the station announces our arrival at Caernarfon, or Caernarvon, as British Railways spelt it. The railway companies showed cavalier disregard for rendering Welsh names accurately, and the original spelling of the station's name was Carnarvon, later adjusted to the Caernarvon seen here on BR's enamel board and photographed by one of the authors in 1972.

The railway history of Caernarfon is quite complicated and encompasses three stations in all. The machinations of Victorian railway companies often led to complexity, even in quite small places such as Caernarfon. The first station in the town was the original terminus of the Bangor & Carnarvon Railway. The single track opened to Caernarfon for passenger services on 1st July 1852; goods services followed on 10th August 1852, all trains being worked by the LNWR. In 1853 there were four trains to and from Bangor on weekdays and two on Sundays, and from 1st October 1854 the service was used to carry mail from Caernarfon.

On 29th July 1862 the Carnarvonshire Railway was incorporated with powers to build a railway from Caernarfon to Porthmadog. The line opened between Afon Wen and Pant, 1½ miles to the south of Caernarfon, on 2nd September 1867 and was transferred to the LNWR in March 1869. Another line opened from Llanberis to Caernarfon on 1st July 1869, built by the Carnarvon & Llanberis Railway, and this had a temporary terminus on the south side of Caernarfon known as Carnarvon Morfa. The town thus had three terminal stations, all of which were worked by the LNWR. As early as 5th July 1865 a link called the Carnarvon Town Line had been authorised to connect all of the railways, which involved extending the Afon Wen line to meet the Llanberis line and the building of a 163yd tunnel under the town. This enabled the two lines that approached from the south to form an end-on junction with the B&CR just south of Carnarvon station. The line was first used by goods services in August 1870 and by passenger trains from January 1871 and this completed

the through route from Bangor to Afon Wen. The attraction of Caernarfon was that it offered a quay from which slate could be transported, and this is shown clearly in early illustrations from the time when slate was an important element of the local economy.

CAERNARFON

Extensive handling facilities for slate were developed in the shadow of Caernarfon castle, one of the most historic sites in Wales. A Victorian photograph shows the juxtaposition of sailing vessels and the railway wagons that brought down the dressed slate from the quarries. With good reason it was said at the time, that 'Welsh slate roofed the world'. Much would have come via the North Wales Narrow Gauge Railway from the Bryngwyn Quarries then transhipped into standard gauge wagons at Dinas for onward movement by the LNWR to Caernarfon. Other loads came from the Nantlle quarries.

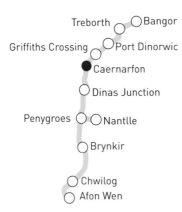

Treborth — Bangor
Griffiths Crossing — Port Dinorwic
Caernarfon
Dinas Junction
Penygroes — Nantlle
Brynkir
Chwilog
Afon Wen

SPECIAL 2nd-CHEAP DAY
Caernarvon
to
PENYCHAIN
via Afon Wen
(M)   Fare 5/3
For conditions see over

SPECIAL CHEAP DAY 2nd
Penychain
to
CAERNARVON
via Afon Wen
Fare 5/3   (M)
For conditions see over

2nd-SINGLE SINGLE-2nd
Penygroes to
Penygroes
Caernarvon
Penygroes
Caernarvon
CAERNARVON
(M)   1/9   Fare   1/9   (M)
For conditions see over   For conditions see over

22575 Carnarvon. Castle and Slate Quay.

An early postcard view shows a passenger train heading for Llanberis with the quay on the left together with the extensive stack yards and sidings. The view was taken from No 3 Box, which closed in 1910. The train would have just passed through the tunnel under Caernarfon town centre that completed the link between Bangor and Afon Wen.

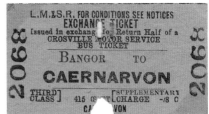

L.M.&S.R. FOR CONDITIONS SEE NOTICES
EXCHANGE TICKET
Issued in exchange for Return Half of a
CROSVILLE MOTOR SERVICE
BUS TICKET
BANGOR   TO
CAERNARVON
THIRD
CLASS]   415 (S)T CHARGE -/8 C
SUPPLEMENTARY
CAERNARVON
2068

Once the route between Bangor and Afon Wen was complete and Carnarvon was a through station, alterations were necessary and these included the lengthening of a platform and the creation of bay platforms at both ends. The original goods shed was demolished and a new one built on a different site in the yard. Stables for eight horses were provided together with storerooms for hay and tack. A new locomotive depot with a 42ft turntable was built. This was numbered 21C by the LNWR. Even though it housed 11 locomotives in 1921, it closed 10 years later on 14th September 1931. One of the features at Caernarfon was the old LNWR timber signal box with 68 levers called Carnarvon No 1, sited to the north of the station. It became notorious to railway employees because of its infestation of alarmingly sized rats and was known as the Rat Hole.

In the photograph below we see an unusual and powerful LMS 4-6-2 tank No 6955 blowing off steam on arrival at Caernarvon station with a train from Bangor. The train consists of 3 vintage 6-wheeled carriages and behind the train one can see the canopies over the platform and footbridge. Much of this weather protection was removed in the 1950s.

Butlin's holiday camp at Penychain played an important role in the later history of the line. In an interesting shot we see Ivatt class 4MT 2-6-0 No 43052 passing through Caernarfon with a special load. It was moving ex-LMS Princess Royal class No 6203 *Princess Margaret Rose* from Crewe works to the Butlin's camp for static display in May 1963. The two barrier wagons were included in the train to avoid excessive weight on bridges.

Goods traffic always made an important contribution to the revenues of the line. Here we see BR Standard class 4 4-6-0 No 75029 leaving the goods yard at Caernarfon under clear signals as it joins the main line with the pick-up goods to Menai Bridge. The low angle of the sun highlights the locomotive and its train, setting it off against the backdrop of the Menai Strait.

A photograph taken from the footplate of Stanier class 5 No 44711 gives a clear view of the castle. The locomotive on this occasion was running tender first towards Caernarfon with a goods train from Llanberis in the mid-1960s. The buildings that can be glimpsed on the left are part of the old De Winton works, an engineering firm famous for its distinctive vertical boiler quarry engines. The two-arm bracket signal holds the two Up distant signals for Caernarvon No 2 Box. The line on the left is the Afon Wen line while on the right is the Llanberis line, with the split taking place at the end of Caernarfon station. Here the arrangement gives the impression that the locomotive is running 'wrong line'. The picture was taken close to the site of the present Welsh Highland Railway station.

The development of railways had a dramatic impact on agriculture in Wales just as it did for the rest of the United Kingdom. Before the advent of the railways, drovers would have driven the animals to London, a trade that was rendered obsolete. After the 1870s, no Welsh cattle arrived in London other than by railway wagon. As the 20th century wore on, motor transport made inroads into this traffic just as it did into others. The very last cattle train to run in Britain ran from Holyhead to York on 30th November 1975. One unusual duty carried out at Caernarfon was the cleaning and servicing of the cattle trucks used on such services out of Holyhead. The washing out was usually carried out from the old wooden excursion platform (Platform 6). Here we see Sulzer Type 2 D5084 (later renumbered 24 084) descending the incline from Caernarfon to Menai Bridge with a train of cattle wagons in 1968. Freight traffic on the line was finally limited to a twice weekly trip and it ended altogether in 1969.

South of Caernarfon, the branch for Llanberis curved off to the east. The Carnarvon & Llanberis Railway, authorised on 14th July 1864, ran from Carnarvon Morfa to Llanberis and was 9 miles in length. Although work began on 15th September 1864, progress was slow as the company struggled financially from the start and work on the line stopped completely during the financial crisis of 1866. The LNWR, always keen to swallow up a minnow, offered to buy the line and complete it. It was an offer that could not be refused, since they used the threat of promoting an alternative scheme of their own as leverage. A compromise was reached whereby the line became a joint concern and the branch opened for both goods and passenger services on 1st July 1869. The LNWR took over the line completely the following year. The Llanberis branch remained in use for regular passenger services until 22nd November 1930 and for excursions until October 1963. The last goods train ran on 7th September 1964, and track lifting began in February 1965.

The first of our pictures of the branch was taken from a carriage on a rail tour as it passed through Pontrhythallt, an intermediate station that served a nearby village, and a number of the locals had turned out to see the train. The yard was still in use for freight and a rather weathered loading gauge frames the station buildings, which survive as a private dwelling.

A joint railtour by the Stephenson and Manchester Locomotive Societies stands at Llanberis, hauled by a pair of Ivatt 2-6-2 tank engines. The numbers were 41200 (the first of the class and a favourite at Bangor Shed) and 41234, and the trip took place on 20th October 1963. The summit of Snowdon dominates the skyline. The platform and track remained neat and tidy despite having been closed to regular passenger services for some 30 years when the picture was taken. The footbridge seen in the background gave access from the town to the lakeside over the railway.

One of the last goods trains to work the branch was photographed bursting out of a short cutting and from under the road bridge after just departing from Cwm y Glo station with a goods train for Caernarfon in 1964. The locomotive was BR 4-6-0 No 75009.

DINAS JUNCTION

Returning to the main line, the next station south of Caernarfon was Dinas Junction, which was once again a station serving only a small local population. It was a slightly later addition to the route, opening on 15th August 1877. Its purpose was to act as an interchange with the North Wales Narrow Gauge Railway that had opened its 2ft gauge line into Dinas on 21st May 1877, with passengers being carried on it from 15th August 1877. The station's interchange status ensured it was reasonably well provided with facilities. Indeed, as traffic levels increased, further improvements were made and a passing loop was installed together with a second platform. Our photograph (see page 44) was taken in the early years of the 20th century and gives a good impression of the layout. We have an LNWR train facing us on the Down platform heading for Afon Wen. This was, in effect, an island

platform, as the NWNGR terminated on its eastern side. Whilst the LNWR side was an actual brick-faced platform, the NWNGR line was at ground level, its rails ballasted up to rail level with cinders. The photograph also shows the goods shed and some interchange sidings on the right that facilitated the transfer of freight between the different gauges. Between the LNWR and the NWNGR lines was a single-storey stone station building with a pitched roof of slate. The building was the property of the NWNGR but it provided passenger facilities for both lines. On the Up platform a train for Caernarfon is seen awaiting departure. On that platform the LNWR signal box of brick and timber construction housed a Webb-type frame. On the south side of the line the NWNGR had an engine shed and facilities for the storage of passenger coaches.

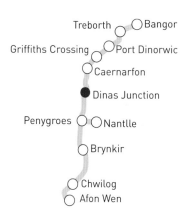

What is striking about the illustration is that it shows a hive of railway activity but a remarkable dearth of passengers; in fact, the railway staff outnumber the paying customers. At the time of opening Dinas Junction was served by LNWR trains running between Afon Wen and Bangor and by NWNGR trains running to and from south Snowdon. According to the Bradshaw timetable for December 1895 there were 14 Monday to Friday departures and 20 on Saturday. Six of these trains left for Snowdon and Bryngwyn along NWNGR metals.

In July 1912 Dinas was renamed Dinas Junction and was the only station on the line to be honoured with this suffix. The NWNGR was not a financial success, especially after an abortive attempt had been made to extend the line to Porthmadog by creating a new section of railway and using an existing line, the Croesor Tramway. Passenger services were suspended at the end of 1913, and on 1st November 1916 the line closed.

On 31st July 1922 the NWNGR became part of the Welsh Highland Railway, which also took over the Croesor Tramway and built a line from it to Rhyd Ddu via Beddgelert. The line to Porthmadog via Beddgelert opened for traffic on 1st June 1923 and from that time passengers could travel between Dinas Junction and Porthmadog via Beddgelert. The WHR soon found itself in financial difficulty since the anticipated mineral traffic did not materialise and passenger numbers were significant only during the brief summer season. The WHR went into receivership in 1927. Passenger services were reduced and became summer-only, and although the LMS advertised the WHR as a day-out opportunity with through tickets being available, the passenger service was withdrawn completely on 28th September 1936. A year later, goods services also ceased. With the end of WHR services passenger numbers at Dinas Junction declined and without the WHR the station no longer justified the suffix 'junction', which was removed from

26th September 1938. The station closed to all business on 10th September 1951, but again it was to enjoy a brief moment of glory and later a rebirth. On 9th August 1963 H M The Queen boarded a train at Dinas that took her to Criccieth to visit her brother-in-law, Anthony Armstrong Jones, Earl of Snowdon. The station was tidied up, with vegetation being cut back and a 6ft strip of tarmac being laid, but there was no ceremony as the Queen was on a private visit. After the closure of the Bangor-Afon Wen line the site became a depot for Gwynedd County Council. The station building and goods shed survived as part of the depot, but the space between the platforms on the former LNWR line was filled in and levelled.

In 1997 work began on the construction of a 'new' WHR between Caernarfon and Dinas using the trackbed of the former LNWR line and the section opened to passenger services on 11th October 1997. Laid as a single line, the WHR was provided with a run-round loop at Dinas on the site of the

former LNWR line, and two platforms were constructed. The original NWNGR station was brought back into use, and the goods shed was developed as a museum. Carriage sheds were built on the site of the former sidings area, east of the line and south of the goods shed. On 7th August 2000 the line was extended to Waunfawr and Dinas became a through station. Further extensions of the line followed in stages, with the final section into Porthmadog opening to regular passenger services in 2011.

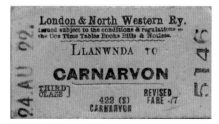

In another of Norman Kneale's evocative footplate shots, we see Dinas station in its 'dormant' phase. After it closed, the station's passing loop and signal box remained in use and are seen here on the right as the locomotive approaches from the north. The engine was ex-LMS 2-6-4 tank engine No 42076.

Travelling south from Dinas Junction, the next station to be reached was Llanwnda. The fact that it was originally called Pwllheli Road was, even by 19th century railway standards, somewhat optimistic, since Pwllheli was some 20 miles away. The excuse was possibly that the road to Pwllheli crossed over the line just to the north of the station and had in fact been slightly diverted to allow for its construction. It was renamed Llanwnda in September 1877 when the new station at Dinas opened a short distance to the north. Dinas was in fact so near that when a signal box was provided at Dinas its distant signal for trains travelling towards Bangor was actually located at the north end of Llanwnda station's platform.

At least Groeslon, the next station in the Down direction, was in the centre of the village from which it took its name, though this proximity did not save it from declining patronage. In this view, Groeslon station is seen after closure with demolition about to start. There is a wagon in the loop waiting to be loaded and a scrap man undoing fishplates. The shelter on the Up platform and the main station buildings on the Down side remain. Behind the crossing gates a class 24 diesel waits to collect the next load of scrap. The station itself survived more-or-less intact, though trackless, until the mid-1970s. In 1975 a haulage road was laid along the trackbed between Llanwnda and Pant Glâs by the MacAlpine company to be used by lorries carrying stone. By 2000 a cycleway and footpath had replaced the haulage road, and a car park was created at the site of what was once Groeslon station.

PENYGROES

just over a mile, from Penygroes to Nantlle, changing it to standard gauge. The converted line became the Nantlle branch and began carrying goods on 1st August 1872, followed by a passenger service on 1 October 1872.

Our picture provides a comprehensive view of the layout. The branch to Nantlle curves off to the left beyond the signal box, on the steps of which the signalman can be seen standing ready for the next train. This 33 lever LNWR box controlled the whole complex layout, which included the branch junction, a passing loop and access to the goods yard. The siding on the left leading to the bay platform was for the Nantlle passenger services, while on the right is the coal yard and cattle dock. Of interest is the gangers' trolley at the end of the platform. The photograph was taken from the footbridge south of the station building.

Penygroes station was situated on the western edge of the village from which it took its name and was a junction for the Nantlle branch. The section of line through Penygroes was originally part of the Nantlle Railway, a horse-drawn tramway opened in 1827 linking slate quarries at Nantlle with Caernarfon's quayside. The Carnarvonshire Railway took over the Nantlle Railway between Penygroes and Caernarfon changing the line to standard gauge, but leaving the section up to Nantlle as a horse-drawn 3ft 6in gauge tramway. In 1870 the LNWR took over a further section of the Nantlle Railway, extending to

NANTLLE

In the 1950s and early 1960s the Nantlle branch became legendary amongst railway enthusiasts since it provided the spectacle of a horse-drawn working. It had the distinction of being the last horse-drawn line on the British Railways network, a wonderful anachronism. Here we see two horses at the exchange sidings in Nantlle station yard pulling loaded wagons containing dressed slate from the quarries. The structure in the background is the water tower for replenishing the standard gauge engines and in the foreground is the wharf where slates were transferred from narrow to standard gauge wagons. At the height of the slate industry more than 40 quarries were recorded in the Nantlle district. Though called Nantlle, the station was actually located on the southern edge of Talysarn village. It was provided with quite an impressive station building. Given that the default weather in the area is rain, it was clad in slate, sides as well as roof. It has survived as a community centre.

Treborth
Bangor
Griffiths Crossing
Port Dinorwic
Caernarfon
Dinas Junction
Penygroes ● ● Nantlle
Brynkir
Chwilog
Afon Wen

On occasion the horses were required to pull a different, rather more animated load, as seen in this view of a railtour taken on 5th May 1957. The two horses were called Prince and Queen. Other 'employees' whose names are recorded were Contractor and Sam.

As regards more conventional passenger services, at the time of opening there was a shuttle between Nantlle and Penygroes with a few trains running to, or starting from, Caernarfon. During the early years of the Great War the LNWR experimented with a petrol-electric railcar on the Nantlle branch. The single-coach railcar was not a success. It could not pull more than its own weight so could not be used for shunting operations at Nantlle between passenger turns as had happened previously; moreover, in the winter its roof-mounted radiators froze and the experiment was deemed a failure. Despite running fairly frequent trains, it proved impossible for the LMS to compete with the buses and the passenger service was withdrawn

on 8th August 1932. Excursion trains continued to visit Nantlle during the 1930s but its primary function was as a goods station. The goods service finally ceased on 2nd December 1963.

Colour photographs of the Nantlle branch are extremely rare. Here on a crisp winter's day in the early 1960s we see the two horses leaving Nantlle station yard with a load of empties on their way back to the quarries. On horse-worked tramways the sleepers were covered by ballast to keep them from fouling the horses' hooves, as is shown here.

BRYNKIR

As the line continued southwards down the Llŷn peninsula towards the coast, the first station to be reached was Pant Glâs. It was an early casualty, closing for business on 7th January 1957, a victim of bus competition. Next stop was Brynkir, and here we see an ex-LMS 2-6-4 tank locomotive arriving bunker first with the pick up freight from Afon Wen. The train, consisting of just two coal wagons and a van, was bound for the yard at Menai Bridge. The station, which was on the western edge of the village of Bryncir from which it took its name, was the scene of an extremely early accident on the line in September 1866, as detailed in the introduction. Also in September, this time in 1920, another accident occurred at Brynkir when at 9.40am an Afon Wen to Bangor passenger train had a head-on collision with a Down goods train from Caernarfon due to a mix-up over signalling. Mercifully no passengers were hurt, though one railwayman lost his life. What the accident highlighted was how busy the intermediate stations could be in the first half of the 20th century. The station staff would not only be engaged with the arrival and departure of trains but also with the handling of merchandise and its onward delivery from the station, and it was someone attempting to do two jobs at once that caused the collision.

One of the ways with which British Railways tried to increase tourist traffic was with the *North Wales Land Cruise* trains that operated with great success for a number of years in the 1950s and early 1960s. The idea was simple. To cater for the holiday trade a series of so-called Land Cruise trains that took holidaymakers on a 152-mile clockwise circular tour of north Wales from Rhyl and the other main resorts was introduced in 1951. By the summer of 1954, there were four Land Cruises operating the circular route that took in the Bangor-Afon Wen line. A feature of the trains was the public address system that allowed a commentary to be broadcast to passengers on their journey. As the handbills proudly announced, the trains were 'specially equipped for actual radio reception for descriptive commentary on the features of interest en route'. Here we see an unidentified LMS class 2 2-6-0 accelerating away from Brynkir with a *North Wales Land Cruise* train heading towards Rhyl in July 1954.

CHWILOG

After passing through two small and rather isolated stations (Ynys and Llangybi), trains to Afon Wen reached Chwilog. The station was an impressive one that once again did not survive closure. The only traces of it that remain are the platform edges that can still be seen within what is now a play area. In the photograph, a solitary passenger waits at Chwilog by the main station buildings in the summer sunshine. To her right are the hand operated crossing gates. The station is neatly maintained with its name picked out on the grassy bank opposite. It is an idyllic scene that recalls a time gone by.

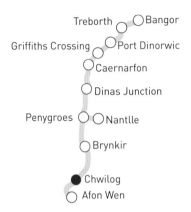

Treborth — Bangor
Griffiths Crossing — Port Dinorwic
Caernarfon
Dinas Junction
Penygroes — Nantlle
Brynkir
Chwilog
Afon Wen

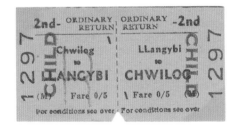

AFON WEN

A feature of the Great Western Railway in Wales was its inheritance of junctions in unlikely, inconvenient, and often inhospitable locations. Afon Wen was a typical example, along with Moat Lane Junction, Talyllyn Junction, Dovey Junction and Barmouth Junction (renamed Morfa Mawddach in 1960). The station was in an isolated location about half-a-mile south of Afon Wen on the very edge of the Irish Sea on the Cambrian Railways' coastal line to Pwllheli. It was assumed from the start that for most passengers it would be an interchange station between the two lines, but access was provided for the locals and visitors via a narrow unmade lane. A footbridge at the western end of the island platform made a connection with the lane, but the bridge was little used, as most of the local population were staff (originally Cambrian employees) housed in railway cottages west of the station site, south of the tracks. The island platform served the Pwllheli trains. On the north side of the line, adjacent to the station, was a house for the stationmaster. Afon Wen had facilities for watering locomotives from two water towers and several areas for disposed of ash and clinker. There was also a turntable on the site in the early days. At the Porthmadog end of the station there were sidings, but no freight handling facilities other than that needed to marshal traffic moving between the two lines. Although the station had facilities, like other Welsh coastal junctions it could be a bleak place during inclement weather as it was so close to the sea. The point of the junction, however, was that it gave access to the Cambrian main line and local services running to all points east and west along their network, which stretched as far east as Oswestry and Whitchurch. For the local population it brought the wider world within reach. As well as local trains, the GWR operated through services to London Paddington. The LMS also offered through coaches to London Euston from Afon Wen but they were not competitive with the GWR services. One interesting point was that passengers travelled on Down trains to Afon Wen but then transferred to Up trains if they carried on travelling in the same direction further south. As regards how the name of the station was written, the LMS and later the London Midland Region of British Railways referred to the station as Afonwen in their timetables, but the Western Region preferred the two-word form of the name, both for timetables and on their totem station nameboards.

Our first photograph of the site gives an impression of just how busy it could be. On the left, ex-LMS 2-6-4 tank engine No 42211 sits on the Bangor line loop while another waits with a return service, and in the centre is the rear of a Cambrian coast line passenger train. It is also a good illustration of the infrastructure, showing the two footbridges, the main station buildings on the island platform and the two water towers. The cars on the left are parked on the grass having been driven up the track on the other side of the fence.

By the 1930s Wales had become a popular holiday destination, and during the summer months there were over one hundred train movements each day at Afon Wen. Scheduled passenger services were reduced during the war but many trains were run for service personnel. Billy Butlin started the construction of his holiday camp a few miles west of Afon Wen in 1939. At the outbreak of hostilities it was taken over by the government for naval use and this generated much railway traffic. After the war the Butlin's camp accepted its first holidaymakers in the summer of 1947 and, as most of the guests reached the camp by rail, special services ran to carry them. The platforms at Afon Wen, as at other stations, were extended to accommodate these longer trains that went directly to the camp, where station facilities were provided at Penychain. The Butlin's camp was a great success, and by the mid-1950s trains were running to Penychain from locations in the northwest, the midlands and even from London. *The Welshman* express service from Euston conveyed through coaches to Pwllheli via the Bangor-Afon Wen line. Here we see Ivatt 2-6-0 No 46430 departing westwards with a holiday service.

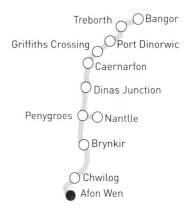

This photograph gives an impression of just how close the station was to the sea – wonderful in the summer, but spare a thought for the railwaymen who had to work there in the winter when a gale was blowing in off the Irish Sea. There was a refreshment room at Afon Wen but it did little business other than with railwaymen and had become notorious for selling poor quality beer. When the author Bill Rear was working for the railway as a fireman, he ventured into the refreshment room on his first visit to Afon Wen. A pint of beer was slammed down in front of him and, being young and inexperienced and not wishing to offend, he drank it – then spent the journey back to Bangor being violently sick and vowing never to go into the refreshment room again.

As we reach the end of our photographic journey down the line from Bangor, it may be worth reminding ourselves of the comic rhyme in the introduction. The reality was that any trip from Bangor to Afon Wen was ponderous and time consuming and only charming to the holiday visitor with time to enjoy the leisurely progress. Billy Butlin gave the line a lease of life and after the Second World War it became busy in the summer months. The winter months were different and the fact that for much of its length the line ran parallel to a main road meant there was an early and steady loss of local traffic to road transport. British Railways might have saved the day when they began to use diesel multiple units on the line in 1958, but in their wisdom the authorities moved them elsewhere and events then took their inevitable course. When we look back at the history of the Bangor-Afon Wen line, we should remember not its decline and closure but what it achieved and see it in a positive light. It provided many Llŷn communities with their first link to the outside world. It gave them an outlet for their agricultural produce and provided vital transport links for the slate industry. It was once an important holiday route and accommodated through coaches from Euston and long trains from Manchester for many years.

In the summer holiday seasons of the late 1950s it was such a delight for a small boy to travel on that it is still remembered with immense pleasure some sixty years later.

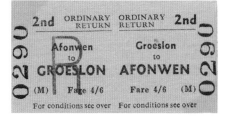

Through services coming off the LMS line had to reverse at Afon Wen and the locos change ends, as the trains faced the wrong way when they came onto the GWR line. Here, from the footplate, we see 2-6-4 tank No 42076 moving slowly towards a Pwllheli-Bangor train at Afon Wen having run round it. The reversing of trains and the running round of locomotives meant Afon Wen was a very busy place during the summer months. Saturday summer trains were frequently ten, and sometimes up to twelve coaches in formation. Local passenger services over the Afon Wen-Menai Bridge line in the 1950s were generally three or four coach formations, although the first train of the day was six coaches, and known as the 'Afon Wen Mail'.

The last passenger service to run into Caernarfon occurred in February 1972 and provides a footnote to our story. The Wirral Railway Circle ran a trip to the town via Holyhead using a DMU. One of the authors was aboard the 6-car set and photographed the event despite the dismal weather.

CREDITS

Lost Lines of Wales – Bangor to Afon Wen

Published in Great Britain in 2018
by Graffeg Limited

Written by Paul Lawton and
David Southern copyright © 2018.
Designed and produced by Graffeg
Limited copyright © 2018

Graffeg Limited, 24 Stradey Park
Business Centre, Mwrwg Road,
Llangennech, Llanelli, Carmarthenshire
SA14 8YP Wales UK Tel 01554 824000
www.graffeg.com

Paul Lawton and David Southern are
hereby identified as the authors of this
work in accordance with section 77 of
the Copyrights, Designs and Patents
Act 1988.

A CIP Catalogue record for this book is
available from the British Library.

ISBN 9781912213115

1 2 3 4 5 6 7 8 9

Photo credits
© Lens of Sutton: pages 12, 52, 55.
© Brian Taylor: pages 15, 16.
© G.W.Goslin – Gresley Society: pages
19, 60.
© E. N. Kneale: pages 20, 23, 28, 30, 36,
37, 38, 39, 42, 46, 53, 62.
© D. Southern collection: pages 24, 31,
34, 63.
© John Ryan – Industrial Railway Society:
page 26.
© Harry Leadbetter collection: page 27.
© Welsh Highland Heritage Group
collection: page 33,
© H. C. Casserley: page 35.
© H. Davies – Photos from the Fifties:
pages 40, 41, 47, 49, 50, 56.
© J. Peden – Industrial Railway Society:
pages 44, 58.
© R. Carpenter: page 48.
© Pat Williams collection: page 51.

Titles in the Lost Lines of Wales series:

Cambrian Coast Line
ISBN 9781909823204

Aberystwyth to Carmarthen
ISBN 9781909823198

Brecon to Newport
ISBN 9781909823181

Ruabon to Barmouth
ISBN 9781909823174

Chester to Holyhead
ISBN 9781912050697

Shrewsbury to Aberystwyth
ISBN 9781912050680

The Mid Wales Line
ISBN 9781912050673

Vale of Neath
ISBN 9781912050666

Rhyl to Corwen
ISBN 9781912213108